AF413241

TAROT VIN

THIS WORKBOOK BELONGS TO

____

NAME

____

EMAIL   PHONE

TAROT CRYSTALS WINE

Welcome to Tarot Vin. Based on the classic Rider-Waite deck, this 22-week workbook is designed to fully immerse you in the Major Arcana archetypes and deepen your connection with Tarot. This journey will also familiarize you with the Minor Arcana, healing crystal properties, key grape varieties, the fundamentals of wine tasting, and your personal palate.

With my background in wine education, journalism, and judging, I noticed early on in my Tarot journey that there is a fascinating relationship between the two. The more I practiced Tarot the more synchronicities I found between the Major Arcana and certain grape varieties. Bridging this connection helped me become better acquainted with each archetype and truly appreciate its intricacies. Additionally, I later became certified in crystal healing and observed a similar dynamic between the archetypes and the healing properties of some of my favorite crystals.

In this workbook, each Major Arcana card includes a crystal and grape variety pairing that embodies its divine nature. Whether you're new to Tarot or an experienced reader, this offers a unique dynamic to your practice as you sip delicious wines along the way.

What's Inside

- Weekly Major Arcana theme with crystal & grape variety pairing
- Spaces for daily card pulls
- Sunday five-card spread that summarizes each Major Arcana
- End-of-week tasting sheet for any wine of your choice
- Reference guide to the Minor Arcana
- Tips on how to taste wine

Keep in Mind…

If you pull that week's Major Arcana pull a second card and consider the message to be amplified. There are several meanings to each card so take the one that resonates most. And remember that there are no bad cards, only good lessons that each one provides. Have compassion for yourself and enjoy the journey.

YOUR JOURNEY

What inspires you to explore Tarot?

____

In what areas of your life would you like to grow with this practice?

____

What intention would you like to set with this workbook?

____

THE
MINOR
ARCANA

WANDS

KING — Leadership & Power
Reversed - Authority & Manipulation

QUEEN — Confidence & Optimism
Reversed - Doubt & Misjudgment

KNIGHT — Ambition & Passion
Reversed - Impulsivity & Negligence

PAGE — Adventure & Opportunity
Reversed - Hastiness & Self-limitation

TEN — Burden & Overwhelm
Reversed - Exhaustion & Delegation

NINE — Endurance & Resilience
Reversed - Paranoia & Stubbornness

EIGHT — Energy & Movement
Reversed - Obstruction & Stagnation

SEVEN — Defense & Protection
Reversed - Hypervigilance & Surrender

SIX — Praise & Victory
Reversed - Egotism & Delay

FIVE — Disagreement & Opposition
Reversed - Compromise & Solution

FOUR — Celebration & Homecoming
Reversed - Transience & Uncertainty

THREE — Expansion & Exploration
Reversed - Obstacle & Restriction

TWO — Decisions & Planning
Reversed - Indecision & Overanalyzing

ACE — Growth & Inspiration
Reversed - Distraction & Blockage

CUPS

KING — Balance & Stability
Reversed - Imbalance & Instability

QUEEN — Compassion & Intuition
Reversed - Detachment & Self-care

KNIGHT — Emotions & Romance
Reversed - Frustration & Jealousy

PAGE — Discovery & Playfulness
Reversed - Foolishness & Immaturity

TEN — Fulfillment & Harmony
Reversed - Disharmony & Tension

NINE — Achievement & Satisfaction
Reversed - Arrogance & Dissatisfaction

EIGHT — Departure & Transition
Reversed - Complacency & Hesitation

SEVEN — Fantasy & Illusion
Reversed - Alignment & Clarity

SIX — Innocence & Nostalgia
Reversed - Attachment & Extrication

FIVE — Defeatism & Grief
Reversed - Acceptance & Solace

FOUR — Apathy & Discontent
Reversed - Awareness & Gratitude

THREE — Joy & Togetherness
Reversed - Excess & Isolation

TWO — Connection & Unity
Reversed - Infatuation & Separation

ACE — Creativity & Love
Reversed - Emptiness & Repression

SWORDS

Air

Gemini | Libra | Aquarius

KING — Integrity & Intellect
Reversed - Corruption & Judgement

QUEEN — Honesty & Lucidity
Reversed - Cynicism & Dishonesty

KNIGHT — Confrontation & Pursuit
Reversed - Aggression & Recklessness

PAGE — Curiosity & Enthusiasm
Reversed - Brashness & Pessimism

TEN — Endings & Victimization
Reversed - Completion & Regeneration

NINE — Anxiety & Despair
Reversed - Coping & Recovery

EIGHT — Imprisonment & Self-restraint
Reversed - Empowerment & Liberation

SEVEN — Deception & Escapism
Reversed - Exposure & Self-deceit

SIX — Healing & Release
Reversed - Baggage & Resistance

FIVE — Conflict & Loss
Reversed - Reconciliation & Remorse

FOUR — Introspection & Recuperation
Reversed - Depletion & Restlessness

THREE — Heartbreak & Trauma
Reversed - Forgiveness & Hope

TWO — Rigidity & Self-defense
Reversed - Confusion & Overload

ACE — Breakthrough & Focus
Reversed - Revision & Vagueness

PENTACLES

Earth

Taurus | Virgo | Capricorn

KING — Abundance & Wealth
Reversed - Greed & Possessiveness

QUEEN — Generosity & Prosperity
Reversed - Intolerance & Materialism

KNIGHT — Determination & Productivity
Reversed - Indifference & Laziness

PAGE — Fascination & Manifestation
Reversed - Naivety & Procrastination

TEN — Fortune & Hidden Magic
Reversed - Dispute & Setback

NINE — Self-reliance & Success
Reversed - Superficiality & Unrestraint

EIGHT — Dedication & Mastery
Reversed - Burnout & Perfectionism

SEVEN — Patience & Persistence
Reversed - Impatience & Rethinking

SIX — Charity & Distribution
Reversed - Division & Inequality

FIVE — Hopelessness & Scarcity
Reversed - Illumination & Revival

FOUR — Control & Frugality
Reversed - Openness & Overspending

THREE — Alliance & Collaboration
Reversed - Competition & Misalignment

TWO — Adaptability & Juggler
Reversed - Disorganization & Struggle

ACE — Beginnings & Plentitude
Reversed - Deficiency & Insecurity

HOW TO TASTE WINE

Tasting wine isn't merely sipping fermented grapes from a pretty glass. It is a sensory experience that blends science, the earth, and the passion of the winemaker.

Here are some tips on how to truly taste wine. That said, no two palates are the same so your experience will be unique to you.

APPEARANCE

In a well-lit setting, tilt the glass against a white backdrop such as a counter, piece of paper, or a wall. Observe the color tone, its depth, and the ring around the edge of the wine. Wine color and depth can range from water-white to opaque purple depending on the grape variety, winemaking methods, and age. For example, a fresh white wine with no oak may appear as pale lemon while a mature red wine with firm tannins may appear as deep garnet.

NOSE

Give the wine a few swirls and then bring the glass to your nose. Observe how distinctly your olfactory receptors can pick up the aromas. If you can easily distinguish aromas it has higher intensity. If you have to search deep into the glass it has lower intensity.

Depending on the style and quality of the wine, you may smell a range of categories such as fruit, flowers, herbs, vegetables, spices, and oak. Mature wines may also develop qualities like honey, dried fruit, leather, earthiness, and more.

PALATE

Acidity is what gives wine its vibrancy and freshness. When acidity is low the wine will feel flabby or dull on the palate. When acidity is high it will induce a mouthwatering sensation on the sides of your tongue. Take a sip and observe the amount and length of this experience.

Sweetness specifically refers to any detectable amount of residual sugar in a wine. This is not to be confused with perceptions of ripe fruit, honey, or other flavors. Most wines are completely dry, but those with any residual sugar will have a noticeable layer of viscosity. The sweeter the wine the more syrupy on the palate.

Intensity of flavor will likely reflect similar characteristics that were detected on the nose. That said, fruit and floral notes can be less expressive on the palate when compared to the nose. Alternatively, flavors such as earthiness, gaminess, and spice can be even more powerful on the palate.

Body refers to the weight that results from alcohol, tannins, and residual sugar in a wine. A simple way to scale this is by comparing wine to different types of fruit juice. For example, lemonade exemplifies a light body while mango juice is full-bodied. Dry white wines with moderate alcohol would have a light body similar to that of lemonade. Red wines with a lot of tannins and alcohol would have considerably more body.

Tannins are specific to red wine but can also be found in white wine that has had extended skin contact. These astringent chemical compounds contribute body as well as texture that can range from plush and velvety to grainy and chewy. Take a small sip and rub your tongue against the roof of your mouth to help determine the level of tannins as well as the wine's overall mouthfeel.

Finish refers to how much flavor you can still taste after each sip. If flavors immediately disappear it has a short finish. If they linger for a bit longer it has a medium finish. A long finish is when the flavors not only linger but continue to evolve into a delicious journey on the palate.

Week of ________

0

THE FOOL

Adventure and exploration. Move forward with courage, optimism, and a free spirit on this brand new journey.

REVERSED
foolhardiness, fearful hesitation

Crystal Pairing
Carnelian

- Confidence
- Optimism
- Vitality

Wine Pairing
Chardonnay

Exploring a wide range of climates and winemaking styles from crisp and minerally to fuller-bodied with oak spice and butter.

MONDAY

CARD

MEANING:

TODAY'S MESSAGE:

TUESDAY

CARD

MEANING:

TODAY'S MESSAGE:

WEDNESDAY

CARD

MEANING:

TODAY'S MESSAGE:

THURSDAY

CARD

MEANING:

TODAY'S MESSAGE:

FRIDAY

CARD

MEANING:

TODAY'S MESSAGE:

SATURDAY

CARD

MEANING:

TODAY'S MESSAGE:

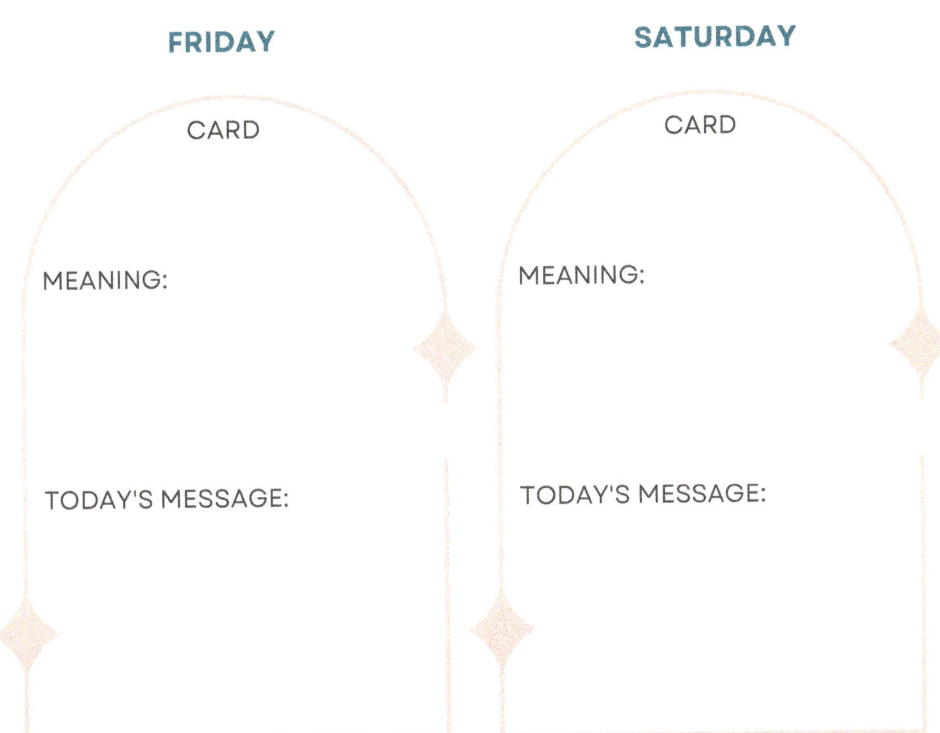

SUNDAY SPREAD

1

New Journey

2

Courage &
Optimism

3

Apprehension

4

Past Experience

5

Proceed with
Confidence

1 CARD:

----

2 CARD:

----

3 CARD:

----

4 CARD:

----

5 CARD:

INTENTION FOR THE NEW WEEK

Wine Notes

Wine / Variety

Producer

Region

Vintage

Price

Alcohol %

Color

Depth

(1) (2) (3) (4) (5)

Clear   Medium   Deep

Aromatic Intensity

(1) (2) (3) (4) (5)

Low   Medium   High

Aromas

Acidity

(1) (2) (3) (4) (5)

Low   Medium   High

Sweetness

(1) (2) (3) (4) (5)

Dry   Medium   Sweet

Body

(1) (2) (3) (4) (5)

Light   Medium   Full

Tannin

(1) (2) (3) (4) (5)

None   Medium   High

Flavor Intensity

(1) (2) (3) (4) (5)

Light   Medium   Full

Finish

(1) (2) (3) (4) (5)

Short   Medium   Long

Flavors

This wine was...

Amazing   Good   Okay   Flawed   Awful

Why?

How does the wine relate to this week's Major Arcana?

Week of _______

THE MAGICIAN

Creation and manifestation. Utilize all the resources at hand and conjure up new energy to reach the highest potential.

REVERSED
manipulation, untapped potential

Crystal Pairing
Selenite

- Connection
- Energy
- Positivity

Wine Pairing
Cabernet Sauvignon

Conducting power by way of tannins, acidity, and density with flavors of blackcurrant, mint, cedar, pepper, and oak spice.

MONDAY

CARD

MEANING:

TODAY'S MESSAGE:

TUESDAY

CARD

MEANING:

TODAY'S MESSAGE:

WEDNESDAY

CARD

MEANING:

TODAY'S MESSAGE:

THURSDAY

CARD

MEANING:

TODAY'S MESSAGE:

FRIDAY

CARD

MEANING:

TODAY'S MESSAGE:

SATURDAY

CARD

MEANING:

TODAY'S MESSAGE:

SUNDAY SPREAD

4

Inspired Action

5

Conduct a Flow
of Energy

3

Energy Blockage

1

Creation

2

Resources

1 CARD:

----

2 CARD:

----

3 CARD:

----

4 CARD:

----

5 CARD:

INTENTION FOR THE NEW WEEK

Wine Notes

Wine / Variety

Vintage

Producer

Price

Region

Alcohol %

Color

Depth

1	2	3	4	5
Clear		Medium		Deep

Aromatic Intensity

1	2	3	4	5
Low		Medium		High

Aromas

Acidity

1	2	3	4	5
Low		Medium		High

Sweetness

1	2	3	4	5
Dry		Medium		Sweet

Body

1	2	3	4	5
Light		Medium		Full

Tannin

1	2	3	4	5
None		Medium		High

Flavor Intensity

1	2	3	4	5
Light		Medium		Full

Finish

1	2	3	4	5
Short		Medium		Long

Flavors

This wine was...

Amazing   Good   Okay   Flawed   Awful

Why?

How does the wine relate to this week's Major Arcana?

Week of ________

THE HIGH PRIESTESS

Intuition and the divine feminine. Tap into the subconscious mind to illuminate life's mysteries and unlock new possibilities.

REVERSED
disconnection, external influences

Crystal Pairing
Unakite

- Intuition
- Patience
- Vision

Wine Pairing
Nebbiolo

Unveiling divine intuition through notes of red fruit, roses, and tar joined by bold tannins, high acidity, and a slightly pale color.

MONDAY

CARD

MEANING:

TODAY'S MESSAGE:

TUESDAY

CARD

MEANING:

TODAY'S MESSAGE:

WEDNESDAY

CARD

MEANING:

TODAY'S MESSAGE:

THURSDAY

CARD

MEANING:

TODAY'S MESSAGE:

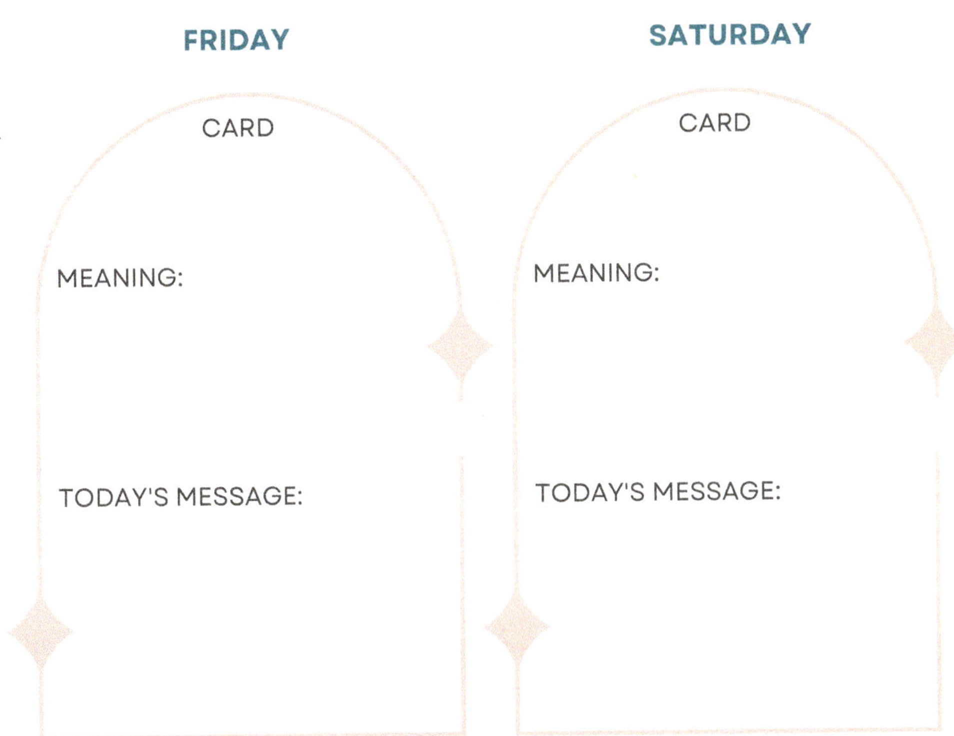

SUNDAY SPREAD

LIFE PURPOSE
THE HIGH PRIESTESS

1

Intuition

2

Duality &
Mysteries

3

External
Influences

4

Divine
Feminine Power

5

Connect to
Higher Self

1 CARD:

2 CARD:

3 CARD:

4 CARD:

5 CARD:

INTENTION FOR THE NEW WEEK

Wine Notes

Wine / Variety

Producer

Region

Vintage

Price

Alcohol %

Color

Depth

(1) (2) (3) (4) (5)

Clear   Medium   Deep

Aromatic Intensity

(1) (2) (3) (4) (5)

Low   Medium   High

Aromas

Acidity

(1) (2) (3) (4) (5)

Low   Medium   High

Sweetness

(1) (2) (3) (4) (5)

Dry   Medium   Sweet

Body

(1) (2) (3) (4) (5)

Light   Medium   Full

Tannin

(1) (2) (3) (4) (5)

None   Medium   High

Flavor Intensity

(1) (2) (3) (4) (5)

Light   Medium   Full

Finish

(1) (2) (3) (4) (5)

Short   Medium   Long

Flavors

This wine was...

😍 Amazing   🙂 Good   😐 Okay   🙁 Flawed   😢 Awful

Why?

How does the wine relate to this week's Major Arcana?

Week of ________

THE EMPRESS

Abundance and sensuality. Nurture the divine feminine energy through self-love, passion, and creative expression.

REVERSED
overindulgence, creative blockage

Crystal Pairing
Malachite

- Abundance
- Prosperity
- Sensuality

Wine Pairing
Viognier

A vigorous medley of ripe stone fruit, fresh herbs, and honeysuckle to suit its plump mouthfeel and underlying texture.

MONDAY

CARD

MEANING:

TODAY'S MESSAGE:

TUESDAY

CARD

MEANING:

TODAY'S MESSAGE:

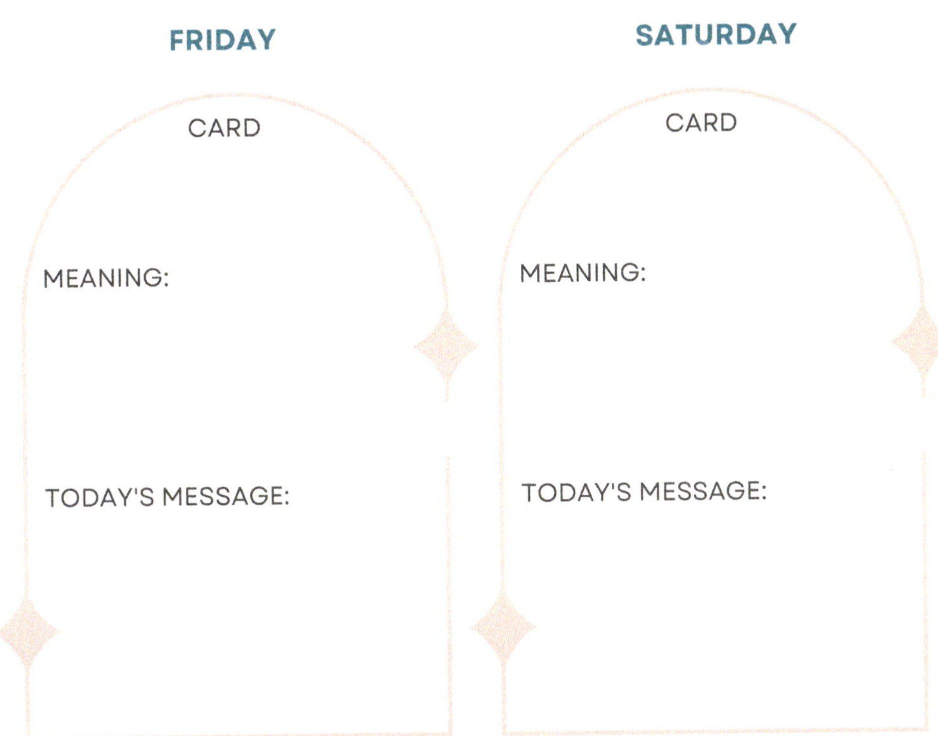

WEDNESDAY

CARD

MEANING:

TODAY'S MESSAGE:

THURSDAY

CARD

MEANING:

TODAY'S MESSAGE:

FRIDAY

CARD

MEANING:

TODAY'S MESSAGE:

SATURDAY

CARD

MEANING:

TODAY'S MESSAGE:

SUNDAY SPREAD

THE EMPRESS

1

Passion & Sensuality

5

Be Receptive to Love

2

Abundance

4

Nurture & Femininity

3

Overdependence

INTENTION FOR THE NEW WEEK

Wine Notes

Wine / Variety

Producer

Region

Vintage

Price

Alcohol %

Color

Depth

| 1 | 2 | 3 | 4 | 5 |

Clear | Medium | Deep

Aromatic Intensity

| 1 | 2 | 3 | 4 | 5 |

Low | Medium | High

Aromas

Acidity

| 1 | 2 | 3 | 4 | 5 |

Low | Medium | High

Sweetness

| 1 | 2 | 3 | 4 | 5 |

Dry | Medium | Sweet

Body

| 1 | 2 | 3 | 4 | 5 |

Light | Medium | Full

Tannin

| 1 | 2 | 3 | 4 | 5 |

None | Medium | High

Flavor Intensity

| 1 | 2 | 3 | 4 | 5 |

Light | Medium | Full

Finish

| 1 | 2 | 3 | 4 | 5 |

Short | Medium | Long

Flavors

This wine was...

Amazing   Good   Okay   Flawed   Awful

Why?

How does the wine relate to this week's Major Arcana?

Week of _______

IV

THE EMPEROR

Authority and structure. Assert personal power, leadership, and wisdom to create a sense of order and stability.

REVERSED
authoritarian, toxic masculinity

Crystal Pairing
Red Jasper

- Grounding
- Power
- Stamina

Wine Pairing
Cabernet Franc

Providing structure and stability with tannins and acidity along with notes of brambly berries, bell pepper, and graphite.

MONDAY

CARD

MEANING:

TODAY'S MESSAGE:

TUESDAY

CARD

MEANING:

TODAY'S MESSAGE:

WEDNESDAY

CARD

MEANING:

TODAY'S MESSAGE:

THURSDAY

CARD

MEANING:

TODAY'S MESSAGE:

FRIDAY

CARD

MEANING:

TODAY'S MESSAGE:

SATURDAY

CARD

MEANING:

TODAY'S MESSAGE:

SUNDAY SPREAD

4

Personal Power

5

Take Assertive Action

3

Authoritative Power

1

Masculine Energy

2

Structure & Stability

1 CARD:

------

2 CARD:

------

3 CARD:

------

4 CARD:

------

5 CARD:

INTENTION FOR THE NEW WEEK

Wine Notes

Wine / Variety

Producer

Region

Vintage

Price

Alcohol %

Color

Depth

(1) (2) (3) (4) (5)

Clear   Medium   Deep

Aromatic Intensity

(1) (2) (3) (4) (5)

Low   Medium   High

Aromas

Acidity

(1) (2) (3) (4) (5)

Low   Medium   High

Sweetness

(1) (2) (3) (4) (5)

Dry   Medium   Sweet

Body

(1) (2) (3) (4) (5)

Light   Medium   Full

Tannin

(1) (2) (3) (4) (5)

None   Medium   High

Flavor Intensity

(1) (2) (3) (4) (5)

Light   Medium   Full

Finish

(1) (2) (3) (4) (5)

Short   Medium   Long

Flavors

This wine was...

😍 Amazing   🙂 Good   😐 Okay   🙁 Flawed   😢 Awful

Why?

How does the wine relate to this week's Major Arcana?

Week of ________

THE HIEROPHANT

Conformity and the establishment. Seek guidance through formal study of shared values and traditional belief systems.

REVERSED
individualism, wisdom within

Crystal Pairing
Hematite

- Cleansing
- Healing
- Support

Wine Pairing
Grenache

Establishing tradition with older vines that offer a full body with notes of red fruit, herbs, baking spice, and white pepper.

MONDAY

CARD

MEANING:

TODAY'S MESSAGE:

TUESDAY

CARD

MEANING:

TODAY'S MESSAGE:

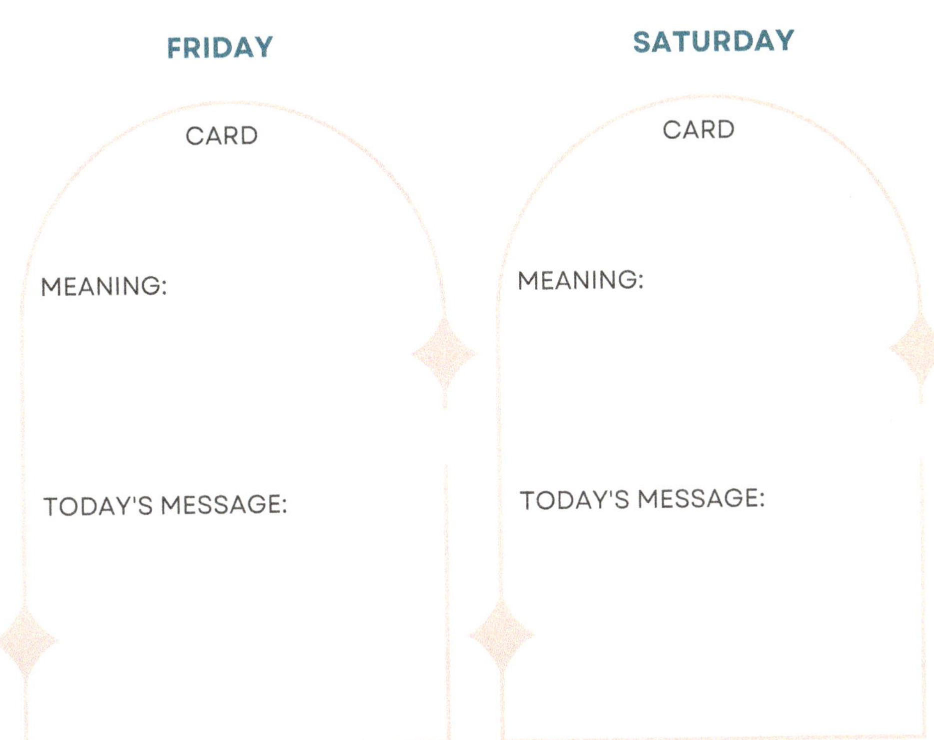

WEDNESDAY

CARD

MEANING:

TODAY'S MESSAGE:

THURSDAY

CARD

MEANING:

TODAY'S MESSAGE:

FRIDAY

CARD

MEANING:

TODAY'S MESSAGE:

SATURDAY

CARD

MEANING:

TODAY'S MESSAGE:

SUNDAY SPREAD

INTENTION FOR THE NEW WEEK

Wine Notes

Wine / Variety

Producer

Region

Vintage

Price

Alcohol %

Color

Depth

1 2 3 4 5

Clear   Medium   Deep

Aromatic Intensity

1 2 3 4 5

Low   Medium   High

Aromas

Acidity

1 2 3 4 5

Low   Medium   High

Sweetness

1 2 3 4 5

Dry   Medium   Sweet

Body

1 2 3 4 5

Light   Medium   Full

Tannin

1 2 3 4 5

None   Medium   High

Flavor Intensity

1 2 3 4 5

Light   Medium   Full

Finish

1 2 3 4 5

Short   Medium   Long

Flavors

This wine was...

Amazing   Good   Okay   Flawed   Awful

Why?

How does the wine relate to this week's Major Arcana?

THE LOVERS

Alignment and unity. Embrace duality and vulnerability through unconditional love, empathy, harmony, and communication.

REVERSED
misalignment, inner conflict

Crystal Pairing
Rose Quartz

- Empathy
- Kindness
- Love

Wine Pairing
Marsanne + Roussanne

A harmonious unity where Marsanne's ripe fruit and round body partners with Roussanne's fresh acidity and flavor intensity.

MONDAY

CARD

MEANING:

TODAY'S MESSAGE:

TUESDAY

CARD

MEANING:

TODAY'S MESSAGE:

WEDNESDAY
CARD
MEANING:
TODAY'S MESSAGE:
THURSDAY
CARD
MEANING:
TODAY'S MESSAGE:

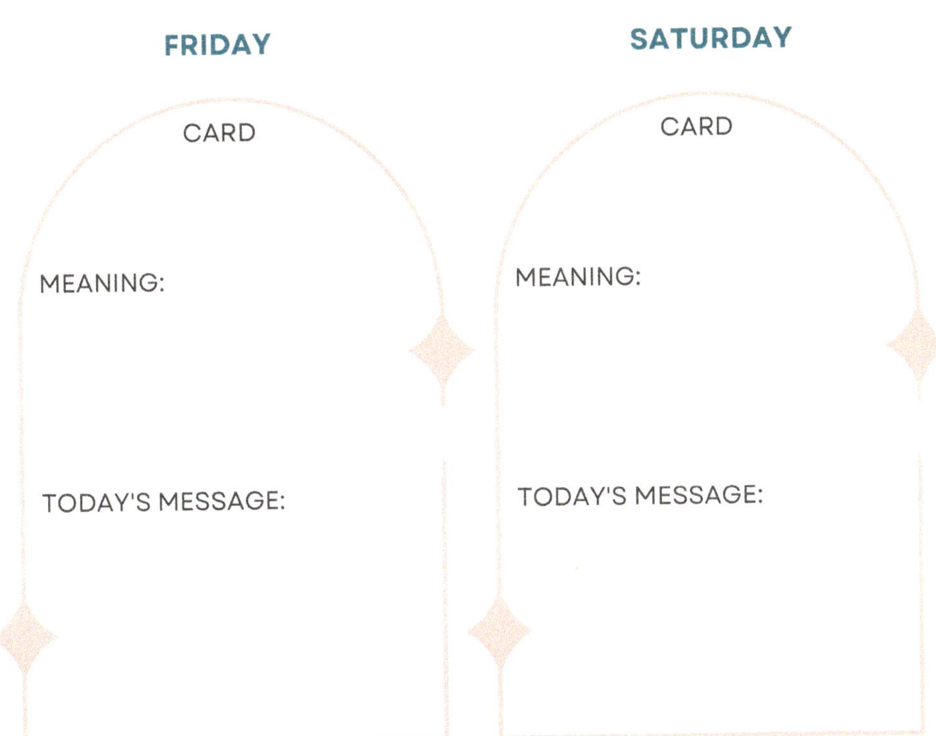
FRIDAY
CARD
MEANING:
TODAY'S MESSAGE:
SATURDAY
CARD
MEANING:
TODAY'S MESSAGE:

SUNDAY SPREAD

1

Unity

5

Embrace Duality

2

Communication

4

Personal Values

3

Misalignment

1 CARD:

2 CARD:

3 CARD:

4 CARD:

5 CARD:

INTENTION FOR THE NEW WEEK

Wine Notes

Wine / Variety

Producer

Region

Vintage

Price

Alcohol %

Color

Depth

(1) (2) (3) (4) (5)

Clear   Medium   Deep

Aromatic Intensity

(1) (2) (3) (4) (5)

Low   Medium   High

Aromas

Acidity

(1) (2) (3) (4) (5)

Low   Medium   High

Sweetness

(1) (2) (3) (4) (5)

Dry   Medium   Sweet

Body

(1) (2) (3) (4) (5)

Light   Medium   Full

Tannin

(1) (2) (3) (4) (5)

None   Medium   High

Flavor Intensity

(1) (2) (3) (4) (5)

Light   Medium   Full

Finish

(1) (2) (3) (4) (5)

Short   Medium   Long

Flavors

This wine was...

😍 Amazing   🙂 Good   😐 Okay   🙁 Flawed   😢 Awful

Why?

How does the wine relate to this week's Major Arcana?

Week of ________

VII

THE CHARIOT

Determination and willpower. Apply a clear sense of focus and intention to take inspired action toward personal success.

REVERSED
reassessment, low motivation

Crystal Pairing
Goldstone

- Ambition
- Empowerment
- Focus

Wine Pairing
Pinot Grigio (Gris)

Focused and thriving in its own skin through diverse styles from lean and crisp to complex and tactile as well as lusciously ageable.

MONDAY

CARD

MEANING:

TODAY'S MESSAGE:

TUESDAY

CARD

MEANING:

TODAY'S MESSAGE:

WEDNESDAY

CARD

MEANING:

TODAY'S MESSAGE:

THURSDAY

CARD

MEANING:

TODAY'S MESSAGE:

FRIDAY

CARD

MEANING:

TODAY'S MESSAGE:

SATURDAY

CARD

MEANING:

TODAY'S MESSAGE:

SUNDAY SPREAD

CREATION
THE CHARIOT

4

Self-Discipline

5

Move Forward
with Confidence

3

Requires
Focus & Planning

1

Determination &
Willpower

2

Action with
Intention

1 CARD:

----

2 CARD:

----

3 CARD:

----

4 CARD:

----

5 CARD:

INTENTION FOR THE NEW WEEK

Wine Notes

Wine / Variety

Vintage

Producer

Price

Region

Alcohol %

Color

Depth

1 2 3 4 5

Clear   Medium   Deep

Aromatic Intensity

1 2 3 4 5

Low   Medium   High

Aromas

Acidity

1 2 3 4 5

Low   Medium   High

Sweetness

1 2 3 4 5

Dry   Medium   Sweet

Body

1 2 3 4 5

Light   Medium   Full

Tannin

1 2 3 4 5

None   Medium   High

Flavor Intensity

1 2 3 4 5

Light   Medium   Full

Finish

1 2 3 4 5

Short   Medium   Long

Flavors

This wine was...

Amazing   Good   Okay   Flawed   Awful

Why?

How does the wine relate to this week's Major Arcana?

Week of ________

STRENGTH

Courage and compassion. Trust inner strength and confront raw emotions with confidence, forgiveness, and love.

REVERSED
self-doubt, depleted energy

Crystal Pairing
Rhodonite

- Compassion
- Forgiveness
- Self-love

Wine Pairing
Pinotage

An arduous crossing of Cinsault and Pinot Noir with older vines offering more depth and elegance of fruit, spice, and earth.

MONDAY

CARD

MEANING:

TODAY'S MESSAGE:

TUESDAY

CARD

MEANING:

TODAY'S MESSAGE:

WEDNESDAY

CARD

MEANING:

TODAY'S MESSAGE:

THURSDAY

CARD

MEANING:

TODAY'S MESSAGE:

FRIDAY

CARD

MEANING:

TODAY'S MESSAGE:

SATURDAY

CARD

MEANING:

TODAY'S MESSAGE:

SUNDAY SPREAD

1

Emotions

5

Channel
Personal Power

2

Acceptance &
Compassion

4

Courage

3

Self-doubt

1 CARD:

----

2 CARD:

----

3 CARD:

----

4 CARD:

----

5 CARD:

INTENTION FOR THE NEW WEEK

Wine Notes

Wine / Variety

Producer

Region

Vintage

Price

Alcohol %

Color

Depth

1 2 3 4 5

Clear   Medium   Deep

Aromatic Intensity

1 2 3 4 5

Low   Medium   High

Aromas

Acidity

1 2 3 4 5

Low   Medium   High

Sweetness

1 2 3 4 5

Dry   Medium   Sweet

Body

1 2 3 4 5

Light   Medium   Full

Tannin

1 2 3 4 5

None   Medium   High

Flavor Intensity

1 2 3 4 5

Light   Medium   Full

Finish

1 2 3 4 5

Short   Medium   Long

Flavors

This wine was...

Amazing   Good   Okay   Flawed   Awful

Why?

How does the wine relate to this week's Major Arcana?

Week of _______

IX

THE HERMIT

Withdrawal and introspection. Detach from the outer world and seek inner wisdom by awakening the subconscious.

REVERSED
recluse, overextended isolation

Crystal Pairing
Zebra Jasper

- Centering
- Clarity
- Yin-yang

Wine Pairing
Malbec

High-altitude offerings of freshness, supple tannins, and concentrated flavors of plum, violet, leather, chocolate, and pepper.

MONDAY

CARD

MEANING:

TODAY'S MESSAGE:

TUESDAY

CARD

MEANING:

TODAY'S MESSAGE:

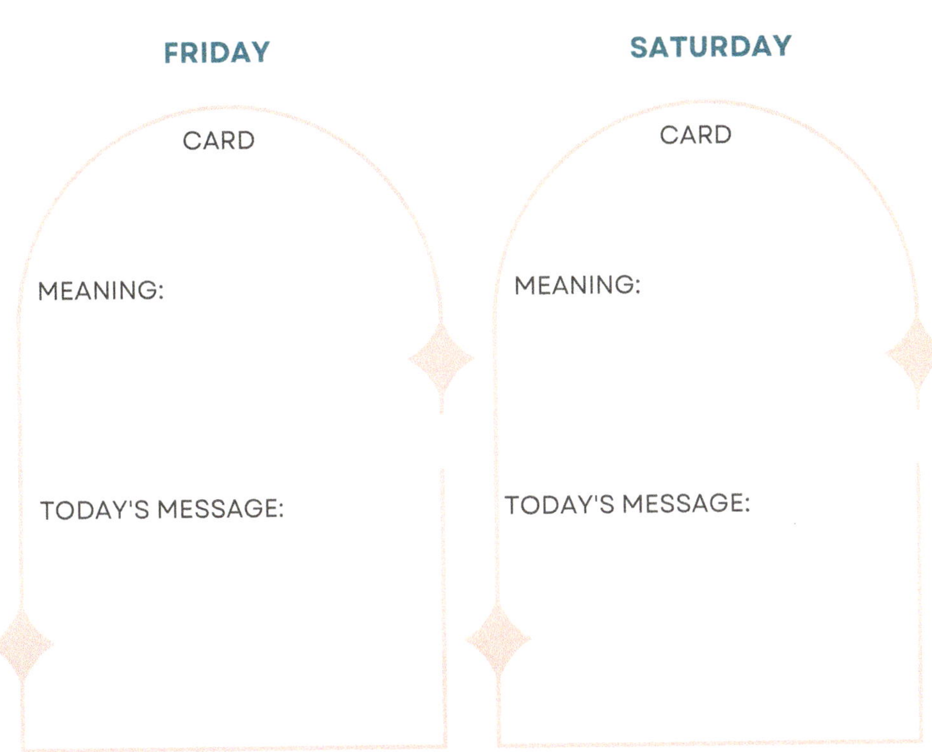

WEDNESDAY

CARD

MEANING:

TODAY'S MESSAGE:

THURSDAY

CARD

MEANING:

TODAY'S MESSAGE:

FRIDAY

CARD

MEANING:

TODAY'S MESSAGE:

SATURDAY

CARD

MEANING:

TODAY'S MESSAGE:

SUNDAY SPREAD

THE HERMIT

1

Withdrawal from the World

2

Deep Introspection

3

Isolation & Loneliness

4

Wisdom & Healing

5

Awaken the Subconscious

1 CARD:

----

2 CARD:

----

3 CARD:

----

4 CARD:

----

5 CARD:

INTENTION FOR THE NEW WEEK

Wine Notes

Wine / Variety

Producer

Region

Vintage

Price

Alcohol %

Color

Depth

| 1 | 2 | 3 | 4 | 5 |
| Clear | | Medium | | Deep |

Aromatic Intensity

| 1 | 2 | 3 | 4 | 5 |
| Low | | Medium | | High |

Aromas

Acidity

| 1 | 2 | 3 | 4 | 5 |
| Low | | Medium | | High |

Sweetness

| 1 | 2 | 3 | 4 | 5 |
| Dry | | Medium | | Sweet |

Body

| 1 | 2 | 3 | 4 | 5 |
| Light | | Medium | | Full |

Tannin

| 1 | 2 | 3 | 4 | 5 |
| None | | Medium | | High |

Flavor Intensity

| 1 | 2 | 3 | 4 | 5 |
| Light | | Medium | | Full |

Finish

| 1 | 2 | 3 | 4 | 5 |
| Short | | Medium | | Long |

Flavors

This wine was...

😍 Amazing   🙂 Good   😐 Okay   🙁 Flawed   😢 Awful

Why?

How does the wine relate to this week's Major Arcana?

Week of ________

WHEEL OF FORTUNE

Karma and constant change. Accept the ever-evolving cycles of life and welcome each new turning point.

REVERSED
helplessness, resisting change

Crystal Pairing
Amazonite

- Harmony
- Luck
- Regeneration

Wine Pairing
Pinot Noir

Demonstrating skill and luck with natural acidity, soft tannins, and dynamic qualities of juicy red fruit, mushroom, and spice.

MONDAY

CARD

MEANING:

TODAY'S MESSAGE:

TUESDAY

CARD

MEANING:

TODAY'S MESSAGE:

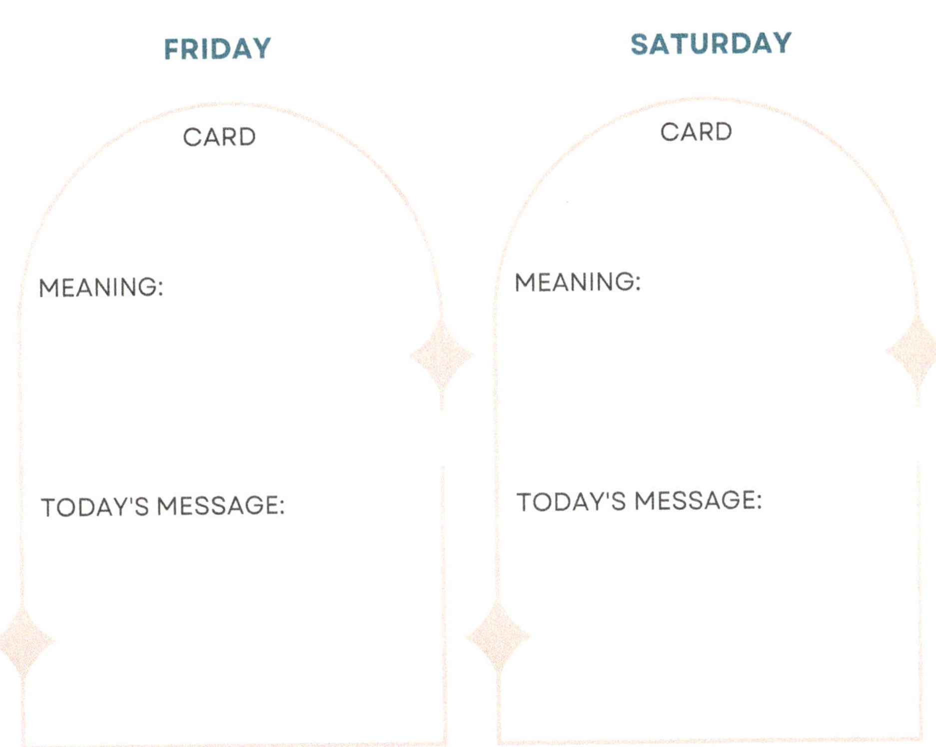

WEDNESDAY

CARD

MEANING:

TODAY'S MESSAGE:

THURSDAY

CARD

MEANING:

TODAY'S MESSAGE:

FRIDAY

CARD

MEANING:

TODAY'S MESSAGE:

SATURDAY

CARD

MEANING:

TODAY'S MESSAGE:

SUNDAY SPREAD

THE RELEASE
WHEEL OF FORTUNE

1

Life Cycles

2

Constant Change

3

Resistance

4

Karmic Lessons

5

Trust in the Universe

1 CARD:

---

2 CARD:

---

3 CARD:

---

4 CARD:

---

5 CARD:

INTENTION FOR THE NEW WEEK

Wine Notes

Wine / Variety ___________________________________

Producer ___________________________________

Region ___________________________________

Vintage ___________________________________

Price ___________________________________

Alcohol % ___________________________________

Color ___________________________________

Depth

(1) (2) (3) (4) (5)

Clear   Medium   Deep

Aromatic Intensity

(1) (2) (3) (4) (5)

Low   Medium   High

Aromas ___________________________________

Acidity

(1) (2) (3) (4) (5)

Low   Medium   High

Sweetness

(1) (2) (3) (4) (5)

Dry   Medium   Sweet

Body

(1) (2) (3) (4) (5)

Light   Medium   Full

Tannin

(1) (2) (3) (4) (5)

None   Medium   High

Flavor Intensity

(1) (2) (3) (4) (5)

Light   Medium   Full

Finish

(1) (2) (3) (4) (5)

Short   Medium   Long

Flavors ___________________________________

This wine was...

Amazing   Good   Okay   Flawed   Awful

Why?

____

How does the wine relate to this week's Major Arcana?

____

____

XI

JUSTICE

Fairness and truth. Take accountability and lead with integrity to help restore balance and egalitarianism.

REVERSED

dishonesty, avoiding accountability

Crystal Pairing
Sodalite

- Balance
- Self-awareness
- Trust

Wine Pairing
Merlot

A balancing act between tannins, body, and acidity that's approachable while offering rich plum, cherry, herbs, and oak spice.

MONDAY

CARD

MEANING:

TODAY'S MESSAGE:

TUESDAY

CARD

MEANING:

TODAY'S MESSAGE:

WEDNESDAY

CARD

MEANING:

TODAY'S MESSAGE:

THURSDAY

CARD

MEANING:

TODAY'S MESSAGE:

FRIDAY

CARD

MEANING:

TODAY'S MESSAGE:

SATURDAY

CARD

MEANING:

TODAY'S MESSAGE:

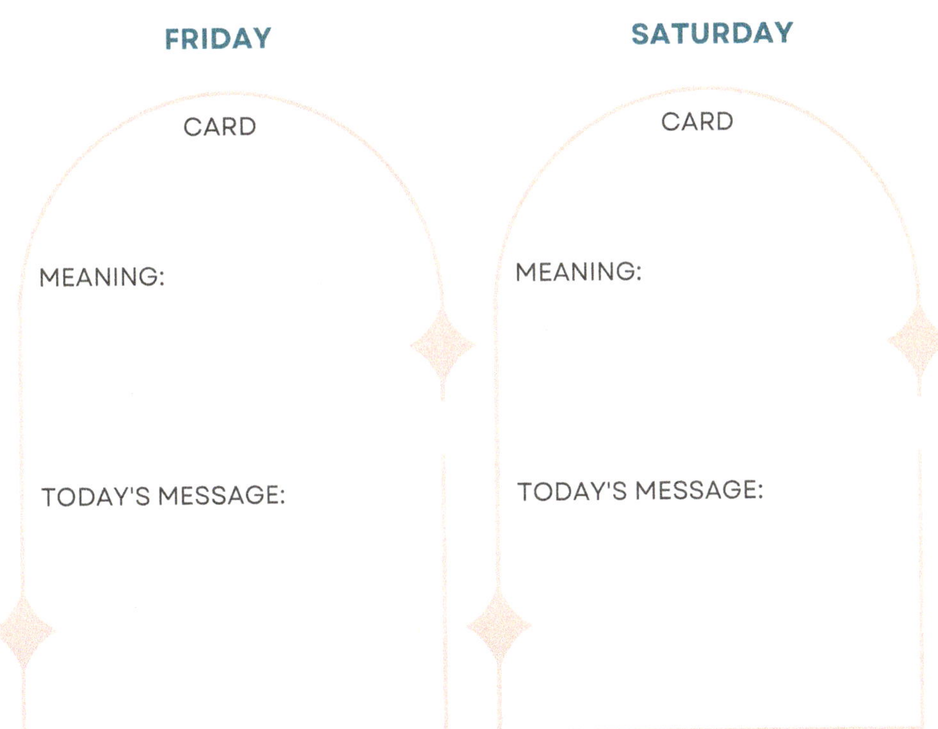

SUNDAY SPREAD

1

Truth & Logic

3

Dishonesty & Challenges

5

Restore Divine Balance

4

Accountability

2

Fairness & Compromise

CARD:

CARD:

CARD:

CARD:

CARD:

INTENTION FOR THE NEW WEEK

Wine Notes

Wine / Variety

Producer

Region

Vintage

Price

Alcohol %

Color

Depth

| 1 | 2 | 3 | 4 | 5 |

Clear   Medium   Deep

Aromatic Intensity

| 1 | 2 | 3 | 4 | 5 |

Low   Medium   High

Aromas

Acidity

| 1 | 2 | 3 | 4 | 5 |

Low   Medium   High

Sweetness

| 1 | 2 | 3 | 4 | 5 |

Dry   Medium   Sweet

Body

| 1 | 2 | 3 | 4 | 5 |

Light   Medium   Full

Tannin

| 1 | 2 | 3 | 4 | 5 |

None   Medium   High

Flavor Intensity

| 1 | 2 | 3 | 4 | 5 |

Light   Medium   Full

Finish

| 1 | 2 | 3 | 4 | 5 |

Short   Medium   Long

Flavors

This wine was...

Amazing   Good   Okay   Flawed   Awful

Why?

How does the wine relate to this week's Major Arcana?

Week of _______

THE HANGED MAN

Respite and contemplation. Release the need for control and surrender to new perspectives and new opportunities.

REVERSED
indecision, restrictive attitude

Crystal Pairing
Amethyst

- Purification
- Self-discovery
- Serenity

Wine Pairing
Sauvignon Blanc

Surrendering to its ornate profile while zippy acidity enlivens distinct flavors of citrus, peach, gooseberry, elderflower, and grass.

MONDAY

CARD

MEANING:

TODAY'S MESSAGE:

TUESDAY

CARD

MEANING:

TODAY'S MESSAGE:

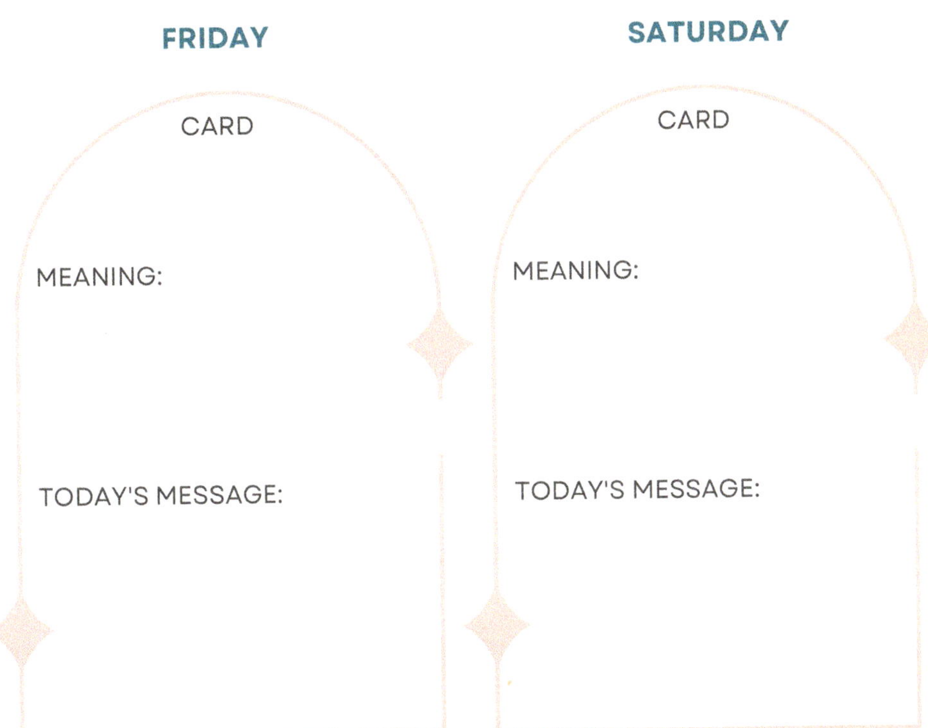

WEDNESDAY
CARD
MEANING:
TODAY'S MESSAGE:

THURSDAY
CARD
MEANING:
TODAY'S MESSAGE:

FRIDAY
CARD
MEANING:
TODAY'S MESSAGE:

SATURDAY
CARD
MEANING:
TODAY'S MESSAGE:

SUNDAY SPREAD

1 CARD:

----

2 CARD:

----

3 CARD:

----

4 CARD:

----

5 CARD:

INTENTION FOR THE NEW WEEK

Wine Notes

Wine / Variety

Producer

Region

Vintage

Price

Alcohol %

Color

Depth

| 1 | 2 | 3 | 4 | 5 |

Clear — Medium — Deep

Aromatic Intensity

| 1 | 2 | 3 | 4 | 5 |

Low — Medium — High

Aromas

Acidity

| 1 | 2 | 3 | 4 | 5 |

Low — Medium — High

Sweetness

| 1 | 2 | 3 | 4 | 5 |

Dry — Medium — Sweet

Body

| 1 | 2 | 3 | 4 | 5 |

Light — Medium — Full

Tannin

| 1 | 2 | 3 | 4 | 5 |

None — Medium — High

Flavor Intensity

| 1 | 2 | 3 | 4 | 5 |

Light — Medium — Full

Finish

| 1 | 2 | 3 | 4 | 5 |

Short — Medium — Long

Flavors

This wine was...

😍 Amazing 🙂 Good 😐 Okay 🙁 Flawed 😢 Awful

Why?

How does the wine relate to this week's Major Arcana?

Week of ________

XIII

DEATH

Endings and transformation. Release fears surrounding change and purge unaligned attachments to allow new life to form.

REVERSED
stagnancy, rigid reluctance

Crystal Pairing
Obsidian

- Growth
- Resilience
- Transformation

Wine Pairing
Gewurztraminer

Transforming its dullness and weight into harmony and grace with notes of ripe apricot, lychee, rose, ginger, pepper, and spice.

MONDAY

CARD

MEANING:

TODAY'S MESSAGE:

TUESDAY

CARD

MEANING:

TODAY'S MESSAGE:

WEDNESDAY

CARD

MEANING:

TODAY'S MESSAGE:

THURSDAY

CARD

MEANING:

TODAY'S MESSAGE:

FRIDAY

CARD

MEANING:

TODAY'S MESSAGE:

SATURDAY

CARD

MEANING:

TODAY'S MESSAGE:
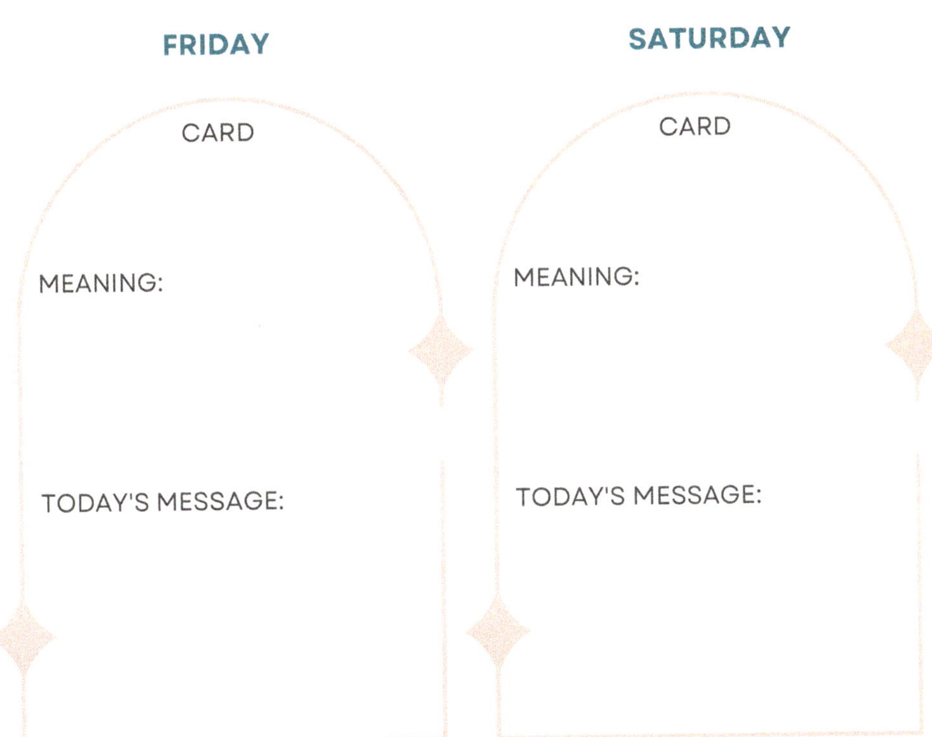

SUNDAY SPREAD

4

Transformation

5

Allow New
Life to Form

3

Stagnation

1

Purity & Love

2

Purging Process

INTENTION FOR THE NEW WEEK

Wine Notes

Wine / Variety

Producer

Region

Vintage

Price

Alcohol %

Color

Depth

| 1 | 2 | 3 | 4 | 5 |

Clear   Medium   Deep

Aromatic Intensity

| 1 | 2 | 3 | 4 | 5 |

Low   Medium   High

Aromas

Acidity

| 1 | 2 | 3 | 4 | 5 |

Low   Medium   High

Sweetness

| 1 | 2 | 3 | 4 | 5 |

Dry   Medium   Sweet

Body

| 1 | 2 | 3 | 4 | 5 |

Light   Medium   Full

Tannin

| 1 | 2 | 3 | 4 | 5 |

None   Medium   High

Flavor Intensity

| 1 | 2 | 3 | 4 | 5 |

Light   Medium   Full

Finish

| 1 | 2 | 3 | 4 | 5 |

Short   Medium   Long

Flavors

This wine was...

Amazing   Good   Okay   Flawed   Awful

Why?

How does the wine relate to this week's Major Arcana?

Week of ________

TEMPERANCE

Harmony and moderation. Embody the essence of alchemy and find purpose through patience, tranquility, and flow.

REVERSED
imbalance, excessive behaviors

Crystal Pairing
Kambaba Jasper

- Alignment
- Security
- Tranquility

Wine Pairing
Tempranillo

Alchemizing ripe grapes into velvety wine with the serenity of plush tannins and hints of strawberry, leather, and oak spice.

MONDAY

CARD

MEANING:

TODAY'S MESSAGE:

TUESDAY

CARD

MEANING:

TODAY'S MESSAGE:

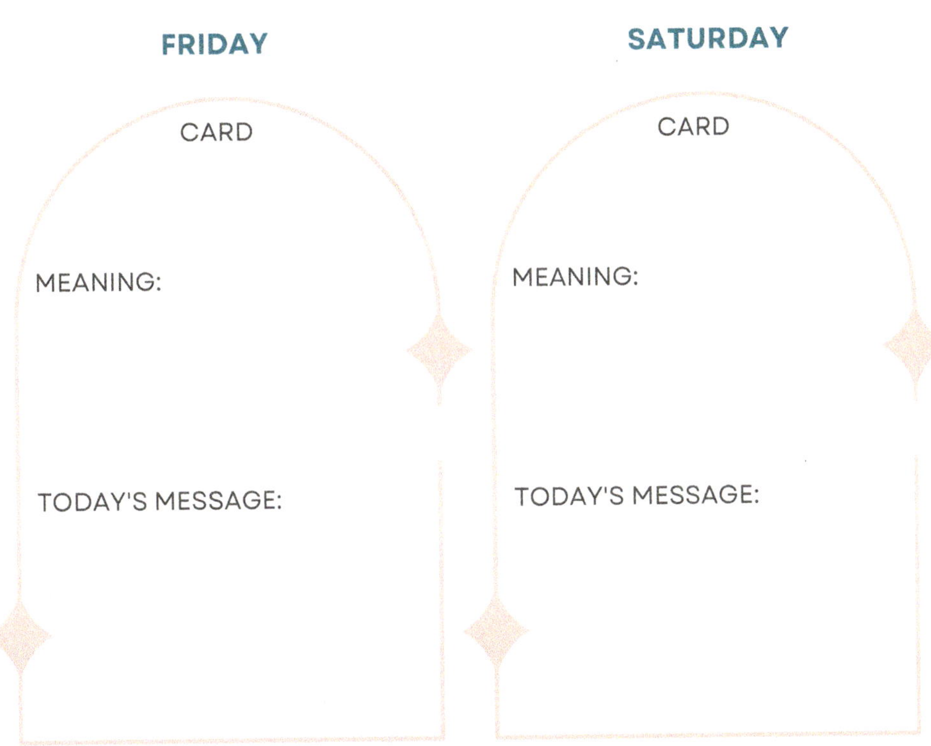

WEDNESDAY

CARD

MEANING:

TODAY'S MESSAGE:

THURSDAY

CARD

MEANING:

TODAY'S MESSAGE:

FRIDAY

CARD

MEANING:

TODAY'S MESSAGE:

SATURDAY

CARD

MEANING:

TODAY'S MESSAGE:

SUNDAY SPREAD

TEMPERANCE

1

**Balance
& Moderation**

2

Patience

3

**Imbalance &
Recklessness**

4

Harmony & Flow

5

**Alchemize Dreams
into Reality**

1 **CARD:**

2 **CARD:**

3 **CARD:**

4 **CARD:**

5 **CARD:**

INTENTION FOR THE NEW WEEK

Wine Notes

Wine / Variety

Producer

Region

Vintage

Price

Alcohol %

Color

Depth

(1) (2) (3) (4) (5)

Clear   Medium   Deep

Aromatic Intensity

(1) (2) (3) (4) (5)

Low   Medium   High

Aromas

Acidity

(1) (2) (3) (4) (5)

Low   Medium   High

Sweetness

(1) (2) (3) (4) (5)

Dry   Medium   Sweet

Body

(1) (2) (3) (4) (5)

Light   Medium   Full

Tannin

(1) (2) (3) (4) (5)

None   Medium   High

Flavor Intensity

(1) (2) (3) (4) (5)

Light   Medium   Full

Finish

(1) (2) (3) (4) (5)

Short   Medium   Long

Flavors

This wine was...

Amazing   Good   Okay   Flawed   Awful

Why?

How does the wine relate to this week's Major Arcana?

XV

THE DEVIL

Illusion and oppression. Break free from toxic situations and pernicious patterns that lead to fear and self-sabotage.

REVERSED
liberation, reclaiming power

Crystal Pairing
Tiger's Eye

- Clairvoyance
- Protection
- Self-assurance

Wine Pairing
Zinfandel

Liberating itself from old stigmas as mature vines offer more even ripening and balance with notes of fruit, licorice, and spice.

MONDAY

CARD

MEANING:

TODAY'S MESSAGE:

TUESDAY

CARD

MEANING:

TODAY'S MESSAGE:

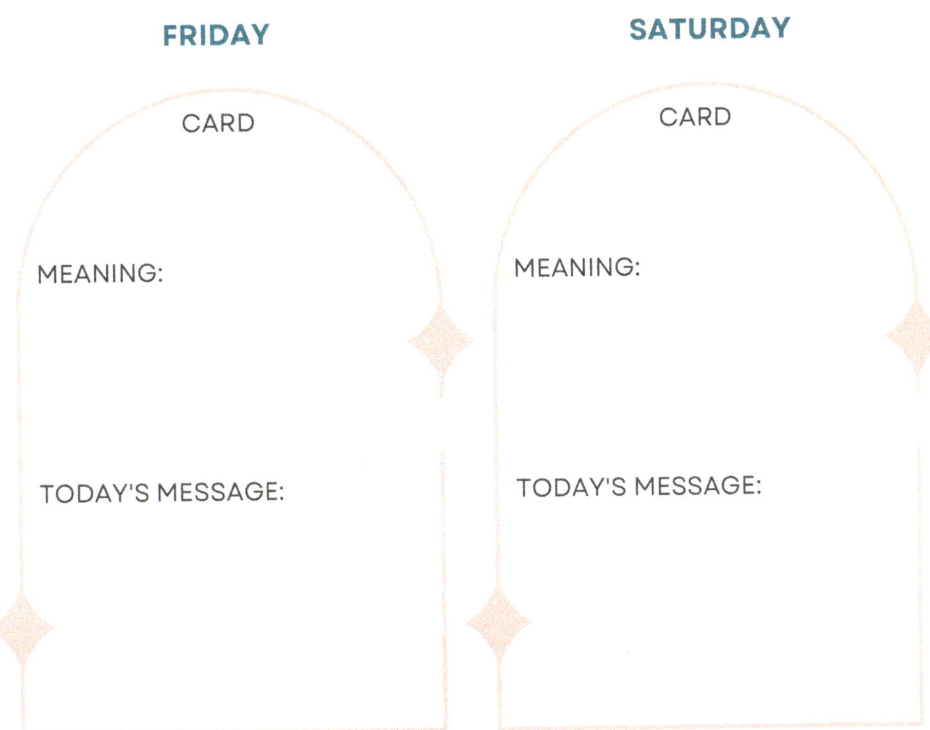

WEDNESDAY

CARD

MEANING:

TODAY'S MESSAGE:

THURSDAY

CARD

MEANING:

TODAY'S MESSAGE:

FRIDAY

CARD

MEANING:

TODAY'S MESSAGE:

SATURDAY

CARD

MEANING:

TODAY'S MESSAGE:

SUNDAY SPREAD

1

Illusion &
Materialism

2

Disempowerment
& Oppression

3

Liberation

4

Attachment &
Co-dependency

5

Release
Limiting Beliefs

1 **CARD:**

----

2 **CARD:**

----

3 **CARD:**

----

4 **CARD:**

----

5 **CARD:**

INTENTION FOR THE NEW WEEK

Wine Notes

Wine / Variety

Producer

Region

Vintage

Price

Alcohol %

Color

Depth

| 1 | 2 | 3 | 4 | 5 |
| Clear | | Medium | | Deep |

Aromatic Intensity

| 1 | 2 | 3 | 4 | 5 |
| Low | | Medium | | High |

Aromas

Acidity

| 1 | 2 | 3 | 4 | 5 |
| Low | | Medium | | High |

Sweetness

| 1 | 2 | 3 | 4 | 5 |
| Dry | | Medium | | Sweet |

Body

| 1 | 2 | 3 | 4 | 5 |
| Light | | Medium | | Full |

Tannin

| 1 | 2 | 3 | 4 | 5 |
| None | | Medium | | High |

Flavor Intensity

| 1 | 2 | 3 | 4 | 5 |
| Light | | Medium | | Full |

Finish

| 1 | 2 | 3 | 4 | 5 |
| Short | | Medium | | Long |

Flavors

This wine was...

Amazing   Good   Okay   Flawed   Awful

Why?

How does the wine relate to this week's Major Arcana?

Week of _______

THE TOWER

Destruction and upheaval. Tear down what no longer serves in order to rebuild toward a new awakening of expansion.

REVERSED
self-imprisonment, private transformation

Crystal Pairing
Tourmaline

- Deflection
- Detoxification
- Motivation

Wine Pairing
Syrah

An upheaval from ripe and fruity to dynamic and age-worthy with notes of black fruit, violet, black pepper, and earthiness.

MONDAY

CARD

MEANING:

TODAY'S MESSAGE:

TUESDAY

CARD

MEANING:

TODAY'S MESSAGE:

WEDNESDAY

CARD

MEANING:

TODAY'S MESSAGE:

THURSDAY

CARD

MEANING:

TODAY'S MESSAGE:

FRIDAY

CARD

MEANING:

TODAY'S MESSAGE:

SATURDAY

CARD

MEANING:

TODAY'S MESSAGE:

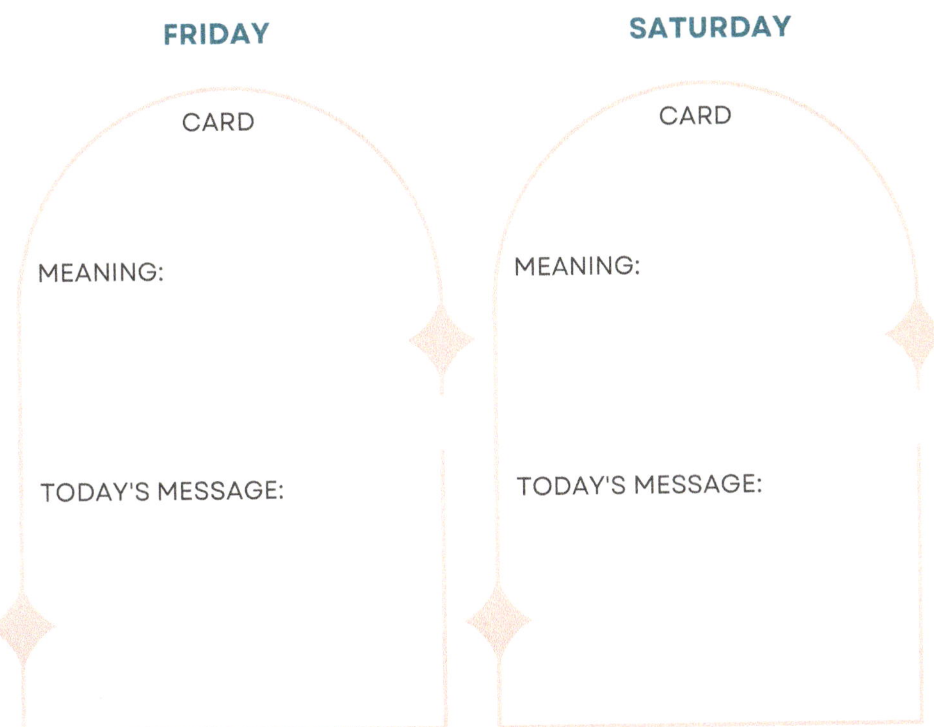

SUNDAY SPREAD

1

Destruction &
Upheaval

2

Loss of Control

3

Self-imprisonment

4

Temporary
Discomfort

5

Rebuild & Expand

1 CARD:

----

2 CARD:

----

3 CARD:

----

4 CARD:

----

5 CARD:

INTENTION FOR THE NEW WEEK

Wine Notes

Wine / Variety

Producer

Region

Vintage

Price

Alcohol %

Color

Depth

1	2	3	4	5
Clear		Medium		Deep

Aromatic Intensity

1	2	3	4	5
Low		Medium		High

Aromas

Acidity

1	2	3	4	5
Low		Medium		High

Sweetness

1	2	3	4	5
Dry		Medium		Sweet

Body

1	2	3	4	5
Light		Medium		Full

Tannin

1	2	3	4	5
None		Medium		High

Flavor Intensity

1	2	3	4	5
Light		Medium		Full

Finish

1	2	3	4	5
Short		Medium		Long

Flavors

This wine was...

😍 Amazing   🙂 Good   😐 Okay   🙁 Flawed   😢 Awful

Why?

How does the wine relate to this week's Major Arcana?

Week of ________

XVII

THE STAR

Hope and rejuvenation. Revitalize after a tempestuous period and allow a new sense of calmness and creativity to flow.

REVERSED
disconnection, feeling despair

Crystal Pairing
Labradorite

- Awakening
- Creativity
- Recovery

Wine Pairing
Grüner Veltliner

Revitalizing the nose and palate with tangy acidity and layers of grapefruit, apricot, dill, radish, white pepper, and minerality .

MONDAY

CARD

MEANING:

TODAY'S MESSAGE:

TUESDAY

CARD

MEANING:

TODAY'S MESSAGE:

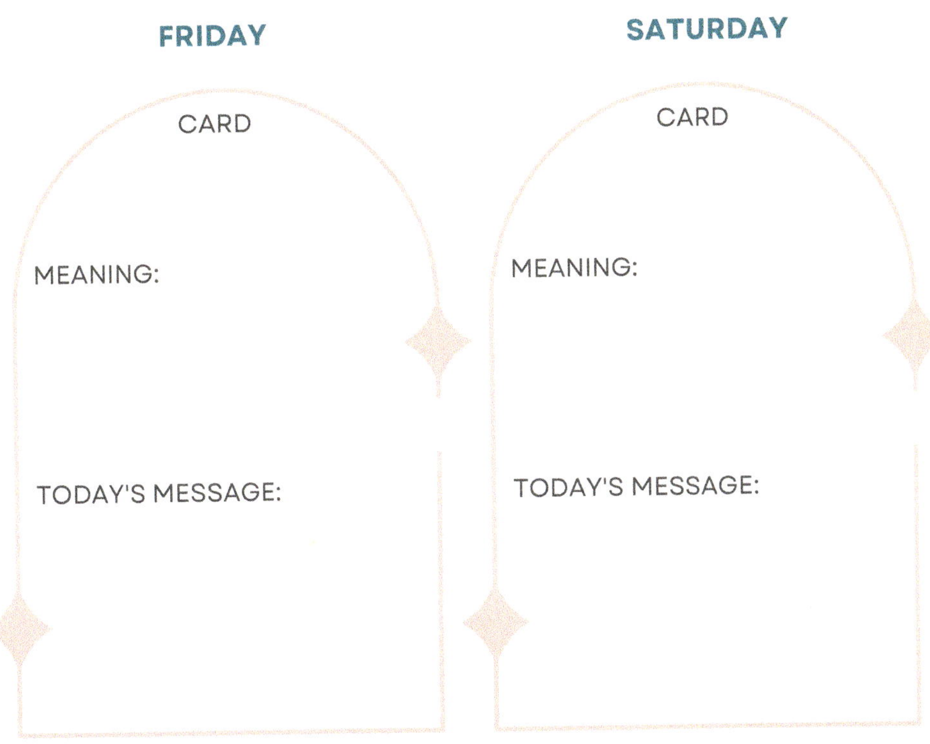

WEDNESDAY

CARD

MEANING:

TODAY'S MESSAGE:

THURSDAY

CARD

MEANING:

TODAY'S MESSAGE:

FRIDAY

CARD

MEANING:

TODAY'S MESSAGE:

SATURDAY

CARD

MEANING:

TODAY'S MESSAGE:

SUNDAY SPREAD

LIFE PURPOSE
THE STAR

1

**Rejuvenation
after the Storm**

2

**Inspired
Creativity**

3

**Test of Faith in
the Universe**

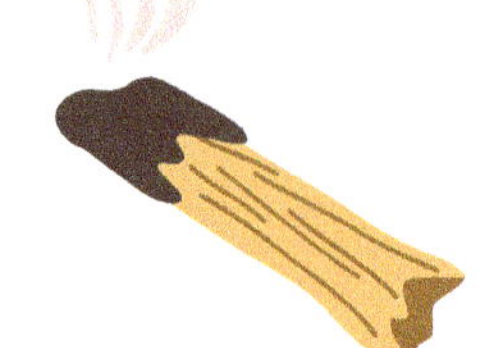

4

Renewal of Hope

5

**Activate the
Unconscious**

1 CARD:

-----

2 CARD:

-----

3 CARD:

-----

4 CARD:

-----

5 CARD:

INTENTION FOR THE NEW WEEK

Wine Notes

Wine / Variety

Producer

Region

Vintage

Price

Alcohol %

Color

Depth

1   2   3   4   5

Clear   Medium   Deep

Aromatic Intensity

1   2   3   4   5

Low   Medium   High

Aromas

Acidity

1   2   3   4   5

Low   Medium   High

Sweetness

1   2   3   4   5

Dry   Medium   Sweet

Body

1   2   3   4   5

Light   Medium   Full

Tannin

1   2   3   4   5

None   Medium   High

Flavor Intensity

1   2   3   4   5

Light   Medium   Full

Finish

1   2   3   4   5

Short   Medium   Long

Flavors

This wine was...

Amazing   Good   Okay   Flawed   Awful

Why?

How does the wine relate to this week's Major Arcana?

Week of _______

THE MOON

Illumination and psychic development. Confront fears, shadows, and uncertainty by exploring the unconscious mind.

REVERSED
self-deception, repressed emotions

Crystal Pairing
Moonstone

- Illumination
- Reflection
- Self-soothing

Wine Pairing
Muscat Blanc à Petits Grains

Confronting lower acidity while soothing the nose and palate with rich notes of grape, orange blossom, rose, and sweet spice.

MONDAY

CARD

MEANING:

TODAY'S MESSAGE:

TUESDAY

CARD

MEANING:

TODAY'S MESSAGE:

WEDNESDAY

CARD

MEANING:

TODAY'S MESSAGE:

THURSDAY

CARD

MEANING:

TODAY'S MESSAGE:

FRIDAY

CARD

MEANING:

TODAY'S MESSAGE:

SATURDAY

CARD

MEANING:

TODAY'S MESSAGE:

SUNDAY SPREAD

1

Illuminated Shadows

2

Emotional Clarity

3

Fear of Uncertainty

4

Intuition

5

Explore the Unconscious

INTENTION FOR THE NEW WEEK

Wine Notes

Wine / Variety ________________________

Vintage ________________

Producer ________________________

Price ________________

Region ________________________

Alcohol % ________________

Color ________________

Depth

(1) (2) (3) (4) (5)

Clear   Medium   Deep

Aromatic Intensity

(1) (2) (3) (4) (5)

Low   Medium   High

Aromas ________________________
____
____

Acidity

(1) (2) (3) (4) (5)

Low   Medium   High

Sweetness

(1) (2) (3) (4) (5)

Dry   Medium   Sweet

Body

(1) (2) (3) (4) (5)

Light   Medium   Full

Tannin

(1) (2) (3) (4) (5)

None   Medium   High

Flavor Intensity

(1) (2) (3) (4) (5)

Light   Medium   Full

Finish

(1) (2) (3) (4) (5)

Short   Medium   Long

Flavors ________________________

- This wine was...

😍 Amazing   🙂 Good   😐 Okay   🙁 Flawed   😢 Awful

- Why?

____

- How does the wine relate to this week's Major Arcana?

____

____

Week of _______

THE SUN

Optimism and vitality. Emerge from the shadow work with a newfound sense of clarity, confidence, warmth, and love.

REVERSED
pessimism, obstructed happiness

Crystal Pairing
Dalmatian Jasper

- Happiness
- Loyalty
- Playfulness

Wine Pairing
Chenin Blanc

Optimizing versatility and vitality with bright acidity, complexity, and eloquent flavors of apple, quince, chamomile, and minerals.

MONDAY

CARD

MEANING:

TODAY'S MESSAGE:

TUESDAY

CARD

MEANING:

TODAY'S MESSAGE:

WEDNESDAY

CARD

MEANING:

TODAY'S MESSAGE:

THURSDAY

CARD

MEANING:

TODAY'S MESSAGE:

FRIDAY

CARD

MEANING:

TODAY'S MESSAGE:

SATURDAY

CARD

MEANING:

TODAY'S MESSAGE:

LOVE
THE SUN

1
Renewed
Vitality

5
Proceed with
Enthusiasm

2
Optimism &
Confidence

4
Warmth &
Gratitude

3
Requires
More Clarity

1 CARD:

----

2 CARD:

----

3 CARD:

----

4 CARD:

----

5 CARD:

INTENTION FOR THE NEW WEEK

Wine Notes

Wine / Variety

Producer

Region

Vintage

Price

Alcohol %

Color

Depth

| 1 | 2 | 3 | 4 | 5 |

Clear   Medium   Deep

Aromatic Intensity

| 1 | 2 | 3 | 4 | 5 |

Low   Medium   High

Aromas

Acidity

| 1 | 2 | 3 | 4 | 5 |

Low   Medium   High

Sweetness

| 1 | 2 | 3 | 4 | 5 |

Dry   Medium   Sweet

Body

| 1 | 2 | 3 | 4 | 5 |

Light   Medium   Full

Tannin

| 1 | 2 | 3 | 4 | 5 |

None   Medium   High

Flavor Intensity

| 1 | 2 | 3 | 4 | 5 |

Light   Medium   Full

Finish

| 1 | 2 | 3 | 4 | 5 |

Short   Medium   Long

Flavors

This wine was...

😍 Amazing   🙂 Good   😐 Okay   🙁 Flawed   😢 Awful

Why?

How does the wine relate to this week's Major Arcana?

Week of _______

JUDGEMENT

Acceptance and spiritual awakening. Rise up to a higher level of consciousness and acquire a greater sense of purpose.

REVERSED
self-evaluation, denying transformation

Crystal Pairing
Snowflake Obsidian

- Guidance
- Synchronicity
- Transcendence

Wine Pairing
Sangiovese

Awakening a true sensory experience through zesty acidity, firm tannins, and nuances of red cherry, tomato leaf, and spice.

MONDAY

CARD

MEANING:

TODAY'S MESSAGE:

TUESDAY

CARD

MEANING:

TODAY'S MESSAGE:

CARD

MEANING:

TODAY'S MESSAGE:

CARD

MEANING:

TODAY'S MESSAGE:

CARD

MEANING:

TODAY'S MESSAGE:

CARD

MEANING:

TODAY'S MESSAGE:

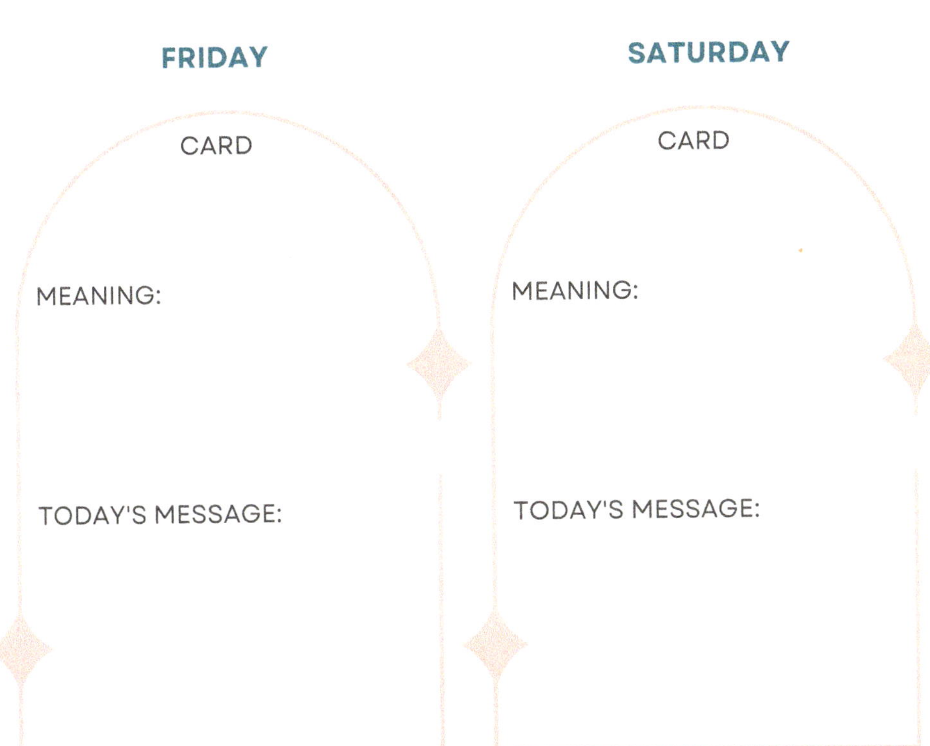

SUNDAY SPREAD

CARD:

CARD:

CARD:

CARD:

CARD:

INTENTION FOR THE NEW WEEK

Wine Notes

Wine / Variety

Producer

Region

Vintage

Price

Alcohol %

Color

Depth

1	2	3	4	5
Clear		Medium		Deep

Aromatic Intensity

1	2	3	4	5
Low		Medium		High

Aromas

Acidity

1	2	3	4	5
Low		Medium		High

Sweetness

1	2	3	4	5
Dry		Medium		Sweet

Body

1	2	3	4	5
Light		Medium		Full

Tannin

1	2	3	4	5
None		Medium		High

Flavor Intensity

1	2	3	4	5
Light		Medium		Full

Finish

1	2	3	4	5
Short		Medium		Long

Flavors

This wine was...

Amazing   Good   Okay   Flawed   Awful

Why?

How does the wine relate to this week's Major Arcana?

Week of ________

THE WORLD

Achievement and fulfillment. Celebrate this major milestone of completion and prepare to embark on a new beginning.

REVERSED
quiescence, incomplete cycle

Crystal Pairing
Clear Quartz

- Amplification
- Enlightenment
- Intention

Wine Pairing
Riesling

Celebrating its fulfillment and vivacious energy with refreshing layers of citrus, nectarine, jasmine, honey, edgy minerals, and petrol.

MONDAY

CARD

MEANING:

TODAY'S MESSAGE:

TUESDAY

CARD

MEANING:

TODAY'S MESSAGE:

WEDNESDAY

CARD

MEANING:

TODAY'S MESSAGE:

THURSDAY

CARD

MEANING:

TODAY'S MESSAGE:

FRIDAY

CARD

MEANING:

TODAY'S MESSAGE:

SATURDAY

CARD

MEANING:

TODAY'S MESSAGE:

SUNDAY SPREAD

1

Major Milestone

2

Intuitive
Understanding

3

Personal
Closure

4

Celebration

5

Embark on a
New Beginning

1 **CARD:**

----

2 **CARD:**

----

3 **CARD:**

----

4 **CARD:**

----

5 **CARD:**

INTENTION FOR THE NEW WEEK

Wine Notes

Wine / Variety

Producer

Region

Vintage

Price

Alcohol %

Color

Depth

(1) (2) (3) (4) (5)

Clear   Medium   Deep

Aromatic Intensity

(1) (2) (3) (4) (5)

Low   Medium   High

Aromas

Acidity

(1) (2) (3) (4) (5)

Low   Medium   High

Sweetness

(1) (2) (3) (4) (5)

Dry   Medium   Sweet

Body

(1) (2) (3) (4) (5)

Light   Medium   Full

Tannin

(1) (2) (3) (4) (5)

None   Medium   High

Flavor Intensity

(1) (2) (3) (4) (5)

Light   Medium   Full

Finish

(1) (2) (3) (4) (5)

Short   Medium   Long

Flavors

- This wine was...

😍 Amazing   🙂 Good   😐 Okay   🙁 Flawed   😫 Awful

- Why?

- How does the wine relate to this week's Major Arcana?

Reflections

Which Major Arcana best represents your current journey?

____

Which crystal do you connect with the most?

____

Which wine or grape variety did you enjoy the most?

____

In what area of your life did you notice the most growth?

____

How would you like to continue exploring Tarot?

____